Eric the Oracle
on Loss and Separation

Relax 'n Learn Teaching Tales

Words by Kate Henderson-Nichol

www.katehendersonnichol.com

Illustrations by Tim Bulmer

www.timbulmerartist.com

Published by Blockley Bank Books

Badger Hill, York, North Yorkshire
First published in Great Britain 2014
Copyright of Kate Henderson-Nichol 2014
Illustrations by Tim Bulmer 2014
Kate Henderson-Nichol and Tim Bulmer have asserted their rights
to be identified as the author and illustrator respectively of this work under
The Copyright, Designs and Patents Act, 1988
British Library Cataloguing in Publication Data
A catalogue record for this book is available from the British Library
All rights reserved. ISBN 978-0-9929157-3-5
Printed in the UK

Born of Tyneside parents, Kate H.N. was brought up with her two brothers in the family home on the edge of Sherwood Forest in Mansfield, Nottinghamshire. Captivated by the magic and mystery of the woodland and its habitants, her active imagination created a world of make believe which became the basis of many a story written to entertain her friends and, in later years, the children of her friends.

An experienced story teller of short tales written for children and young people, Kate H.N. aims to encourage readers and listeners to relax and learn how to help manage their life's challenges and live healthier lifestyles. She applies the metaphor of woodland and river life at Blockley Bank to spell out some clear personal development messages to support children and young people to build their resilience, confidence and self-esteem.

Special thanks to all the support team in Blockley Bank – you know who you are!

Illustrations, Tim Bulmer

Graphic design, Lucy Denham

Editing, Ellie Phipps and Co.

Which ones haven't you read?

Eric the Oracle on:

Self Acceptance

Self-belief and Positive Thinking

More Haste, Less Speed

Loss and Separation

Bullying

Saying 'No' to Strangers

"Hello

and welcome to Relax 'n Learn Teaching Tales.

Just make yourself comfortable and, in your mind, allow yourself to imagine you're walking safely along a riverbank. Notice all the beautiful shapes of the trees and their different colours; hear the leaves whispering about their day here in Blockley Bank. You notice a raised root from the ground that invites you to follow it to the trunk of its tree. Treading carefully, you sit down, making yourself comfortable on the soft dry grass. You can lean back on this willow tree and, not too far away, you notice the light is different from where you're sitting. The harder you look, the dimmer the light seems. The trees are almost in silhouette over there; there's a stillness throughout the woodland. The river silently and gently flows away into the distance, so just relax and learn as the story unfolds, down by the river at Blockley Bank."

Eric the Oracle, the wise, old, warty frog of Blockley Bank, had had a busy few days. His wife, known as the Duchess, had been trying to clear out Eric's wardrobe of some of his older, although still beautiful, waistcoats. He didn't like losing anything, but she announced that now they had more junior frogs to house and feed, they needed the space and the wardrobe had to go. He'd made a start but didn't feel like doing any more, especially in the evening twilight, so he stood up from his deckchair and hopped onto the muddy bank and held onto some grass to pull himself higher to see throughout the woodland.

Just as he did so, his friend Vic the vole popped his head out of his waterside home in the muddy riverbank and asked, *"Eric, what ARE you doing?"* Eric thought that if he talked long enough with Vic it would get him out of clearing his wardrobe. He liked Vic very much (even though he was very nosey), so stopped looking over the bank and replied, *"Oh, I was just wondering if I could see anything because I think an owl family has moved just here into the sycamore tree,"* and pointed over to his right. Eric explained that he'd read in today's Blockleygraph, which was delivered daily by Postie Woodpecker, that there'd been a terrible kerfuffle the day before and the family had no choice but to move. Eric's froglets, who were very much into riverside technology and who had tried to introduce Eric to the Woodland Wide Web's Wingbook and Hooter, had told him that this news was already posted on Wingbook. *"Everyone's hootering each other about what happened!"* he was enthusiastically informed. Eric had no interest in Wingbook or Hooter whatsoever and was confident he could manage perfectly well with the Blockleygraph and listening to the general informative chitchat of the woodland animals and river creatures.

Vic looked solemnly at Eric and in a very quiet voice, said, *"It's really sad. There were two two-legged beings in the wood yesterday, looking at one of the old oak trees that was leaning low over that footpath."* Vic swung his head in the direction of the footpath to illustrate what he was saying. *"We all heard them say it had died from Sudden Oak Death Disease and would have to be felled straight away, without any thought for the owls that live in there."* Leaning now with his back against the riverbank, Eric understood what had happened. He and Vic shook their heads in sympathy and, with a big sigh, Eric gazed out first over the river and then over to the line of trees in the woodland. By now, the moon was shining down onto a cluster of branches of a good-looking sycamore tree where he could see four owls perched, looking lost and forlorn.

All four were clearly very upset; their suitcases bulged with their belongings. Vic mumbled an apology to Eric about not telling him sooner and retreated into his hole to make some tea for them both. Eric thanked his friend, declined the offer of tea but said he'd stay for a while by the grassy bank which was lit up by the light of the moon. Enjoying the moonlight, Eric noticed one of the young owls break away from the family and fly over to the riverbank, just near Eric. He sat down, looking sadly into the distance. Eric watched the young owl as a great big tear like a crystal ball grew and grew from each of the owl's beautiful brown eyes, until there was no more room for them and they fell to the ground, splashing heavily onto the grass.

The young owl looked down, watching his toes get splashed with his tears. All alone, he sat on the grass and leant against the narrow trunk of a birch tree, called the Lady of the Woods. As his head bowed, his beak buried into his feathered chest and more and more huge tears rolled to his feet. Like a waterfall of diamonds in the moonlight, his tears fell to the ground and rolled over the bank. The owl gasped for breath and sobbed out loud, such was his distress.

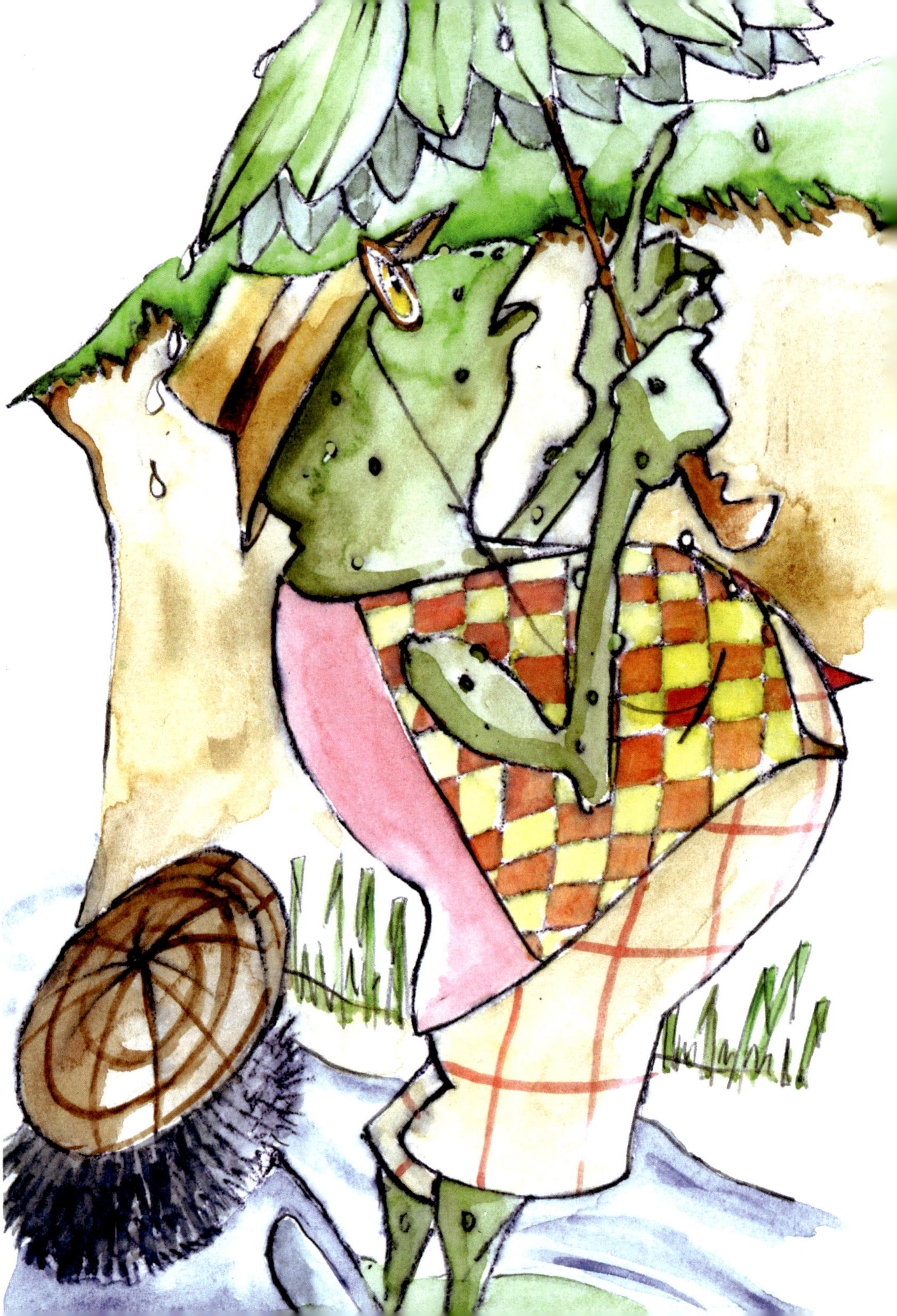

Vic popped his head out from the muddy riverbank wall and offered Eric an umbrella, *"Looks like you'll need this!"* Eric smiled at Vic and gratefully took the umbrella. He carefully put it up to shelter from the shower of tears above him and stretched up to peek over the riverbank so that he could see the distressed owl more clearly. He gently called out, *"Hello there! What sadness, my friend? Whatever's happened? Can I help?"* The owl sniffed loudly and looked around him, swivelling his head a full 360 degrees to see who'd just spoken. Seeing no-one, he wimpered and looked firstly down at his feet, then up to the moonlit sky. He noticed how, in the twilight, it was peppered with twinkling stars waiting to come out fully when the darkness opened them up. *"Why do things have to change?!"* he shouted out, seemingly to nobody. The owl looked back sorrowfully at the river disappearing into the distance. He knew that, beneath the calm surface, the fish went about their business as usual, feeding, silently swimming about, seemingly without a care in the world. Or so he imagined. Everyone else was happily either having their evening food or preparing for sleep and he decided no-one could possibly feel as miserable as he did. Or so he imagined.

Eric could see the owl very clearly now as the moonlight lit up this creature, showing his brown and cream mottled feathery chest and watery brown eyes. Those eyes were filled only with sadness. Eric turned to the river, and keeping hold of his umbrella, hopped back over to sit down in his deckchair of finely woven grasses on his leafy platform. The waterfall of tears had almost dried up as the owl had no more to shed. He was exhausted. He felt alone, with no-one to talk to and no-one to understand. But he'd forgotten that in life there's always someone to talk to, if only you'd look. Now that the owl had caught his breath, Eric folded up his umbrella and threw it back to the bank like a spear, so it landed deeply into the mud ready to be picked up and used if needed. He called out again, *"Over here! Please, come and talk. You look like you could do with a friend!"* The owl turned again to see who was speaking to him and could now see in the moonlight that, not too far from his feet, sitting on a large leafy platform bobbing gently up and down in the water, was a kindly old frog with a smiling face looking up at him.

The owl suddenly realised he was far from alone as the moonlight was reflected in many pairs of eyes belonging to squirrels, spiders, rabbits, birds, hedgehogs, deer and so many more woodland creatures. Even the scales of the fish in the river glinted as they swam closely to the leafy platform. *"This must be Eric the Oracle,"* thought the tearful owl. Everyone sat silently not wanting to scare the distressed owl. They had gathered together to hear what Eric had to say, for he always talked sense and put situations into perspective.

Eric noticed how quiet it was in the woodland and realised that no-one knew what to say or how to say it about this situation with the dead oak tree that had displaced the owl family. The Duchess, who had kept an eye open on Eric whilst clearing his wardrobe, was ahead of the game. Aware that Eric could soon be called upon to speak wise words, she had already prepared his glass of magical dandelion fizzmix, which the woodland animals had delivered, as always, every alternate week when the moon shone dark yellow with orange spots. Crossing his legs, Eric reached down for his glass of magical potion, signalling to the woodland animals and river creatures that great words of wisdom would be spoken. They didn't need Wingbook and Hooter to know what was happening. They knew because they'd noticed the world around them and had seen the two-legged beings with their chainsaws fell and take away their old friend the oak tree who had been so ill and died.

The owl sat up straight, looked towards Eric and tried to smile, but just didn't feel like it. He could barely speak and stuttered, *"Don't b b b b be nice to m m m m me. I can't stop crying. I'm s s s s so embarrassed."* Eric smiled the kindest smile ever and cleared his throat. He didn't need his sunhat on now of course, so instead, two kingfishers flew down from where they were nestled in the leaves of a tree, each picking up an end of a finely woven silk scarf which the spiders had made for Eric. They flew in circles around his head, gently wrapping him in the scarf to keep him warm whilst he spoke his wise words. Very softly, Eric said, *"What an awful time you're all having. It must feel very unfair."* The owl blurted out, *"Why did our home have to die? Why do things have to change? How do we cope without our oak house? We'll never survive!"*

Eric looked up at the owl whose eyes were filling up again with crystal clear tears and suggested, *"I wonder if you could be feeling rather angry underneath all that sadness?"* Without giving the owl time to reply, he continued, *"You're from the Olivante family, aren't you?"* The owl nodded at Eric and replied, *"Yes I'm Tawny Olivante, my twin sister's called Tawnetta. I've just the one sister and she's with our parents. And I AM angry about what's happened to us. I've had to come out because....because..... I have to be brave and I can't be. It's the two-legged beings' fault because they said our home was dead and they chopped it down. It's gone and we'd been there years and now we ...."* Eric put his long spindly finger to his lips and gently said, *"Sshh, it's OK to feel angry and sad all at once, Tawny."* Tawny took a huge deep breath and lifted his head up again and looked at Eric, appreciating that he wasn't being judged or criticised. Everyone in the woodland and river knew that Eric's wise words applied even to the two-legged beings in their world. Everyone was listening as Eric cleared his throat and took a long, noisy slurp of his magical thinking potion. He continued,

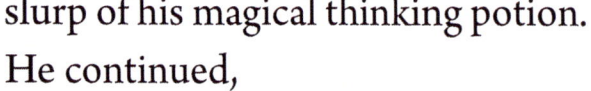

"Tawny, tell me _exactly_ what's made you so sad." The owl looked directly at him and more huge tears welled into his sad eyes. With a few splutters, he answered, "Because it's our home! Our tree is........dead! Why did it have to die? I know it was ill with some disease that the two-leggeds gave a name to, but even so, it was always there for us." Eric looked kindly at the devastated owl. "Oh Tawny, I really can understand what you're feeling. Sadly, your home caught Sudden Oak Death Disease which kills oak trees over quite a short space of time. Sometimes, living things and beings, old and sometimes young, get diseases which means they can't continue to live or, if they do, they have to work out how best to live with it. Losing a life or losing a _way_ of life through illness is hard, but it's the way that life works and we have to find ways to deal with it. _Understanding_ it is a great help."

The woodland animals all looked at each other in the moonlight and nodded in sympathy for the owl family, for every single one of them had experienced this in their own lives and knew how much and for how long it can hurt. Eric took his beautiful willow crafted monocle from his waistcoat pocket and looked through it at the sad owl. *"The oak tree was your home and was a living thing whose life ended. You've had to move, you're grieving for its loss and also for the change in how you live your life. Everything's different now, isn't it, Tawny?"*

Tawny looked at Eric and wondered how on earth this warty old frog could possibly know all this and understand how an owl felt. But he was right. Tawny realised that he was hearing, for real, the gentle wisdom everyone knew and talked about in the woodland. So painful was Tawny's heartache, he desperately wanted the feeling to go away. With great reverence to the Oracle's wisdom, he replied, *"You're right, Sir. I can't find the words to describe how miserable I feel. I'm shocked 'cos it happened so fast in the end. My mind's a mess. I'm devastated, hurt, you're right that I'm angry and I'm scared and even feel guilty* **all at once.** *If I'd respected the tree better maybe it wouldn't have got ill. I wish it would all go away so we can go back to living how we used to in the oak tree. We were all happy then. Now we have no real home, my parents have no time for us any more and I have to be strong for everyone. All my sister's bothered about is where to put her feather drier in the new house!"*

Eric absorbed all that Tawny said, knowing that the terrible pain of grief and loss would lessen and go in time. But there's a process to go through. Re-arranging his silken scarf around his neck, Eric quietly and confidently said to Tawny and the assembled crowd, *"What you're experiencing is neither wrong nor abnormal. In fact, it's right. When you lose something or someone, whether they die (like your oaken home) or change in some way that you have to adapt your life to, or if someone special leaves you to go somewhere else, you're left on your own to carry on and rebuild your life around the gap. Every single one of us reacts in our own way, but there's a pattern of feelings we all go through. As sure as there is sun by day and moon by night, we all feel shocked and numb at first and wonder how we'll ever cope. And we all believe no-one else feels it as badly. After a while, you'll get over the shock and you might feel really lonely, sad and sometimes angry about nothing. Or you might feel guilty that you could have done something differently and stopped it happening. Sometimes you can't sleep or eat properly for ages. Sometimes you just feel terrible and think you'll never be happy again. Hardest of all, those feelings can get you all at once."* Eric paused as he knew he was giving a lot of information for Tawny to hear and absorb. The owl hadn't moved a feather because he was listening so hard. In fact, no-one had moved a feather, fur or scale because they all knew and remembered how they too had lost friends and family either through death or they'd just moved to a different place to live. HOW it hurt. It was as if Eric was in Tawny's head and heart, for everything he said was true.

Eric continued,

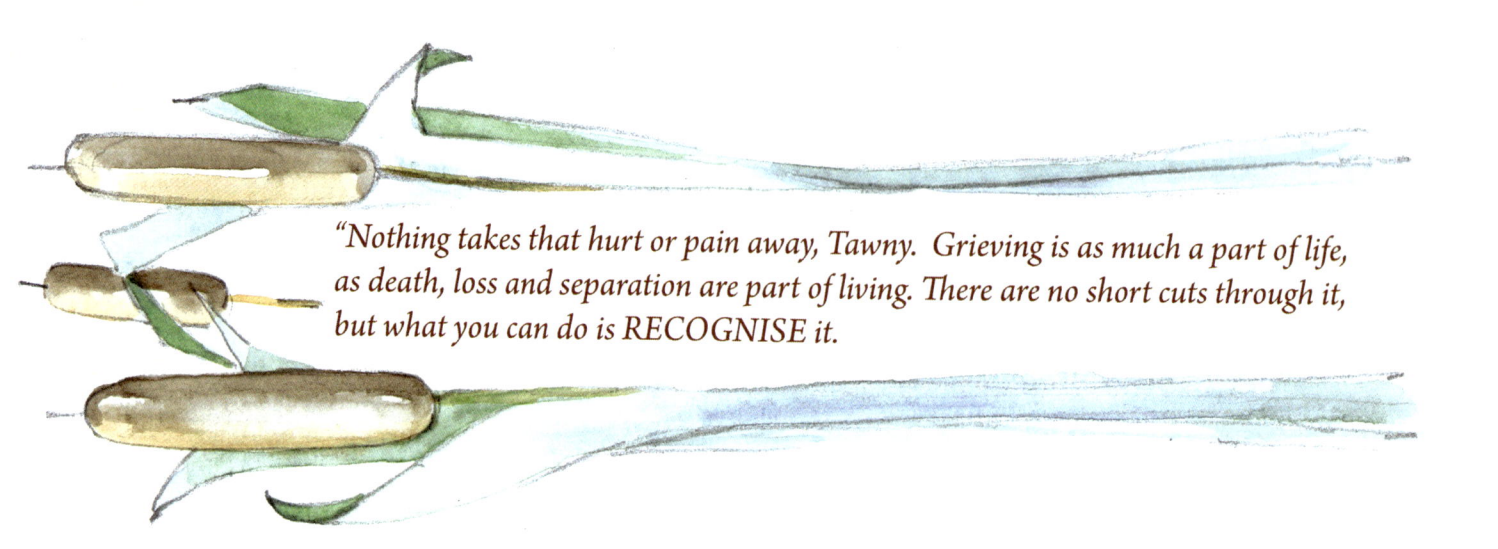

"Nothing takes that hurt or pain away, Tawny. Grieving is as much a part of life, as death, loss and separation are part of living. There are no short cuts through it, but what you can do is RECOGNISE it.

Knowing about the grieving process is the first step towards recognising it and feeling OK again, but you have to give yourself time and space to absorb what's happened to you before you can really apply your knowledge of the grieving process to yourself. Your parents are just as much in shock too. It's not that they don't care or haven't got time for you, it's that they worry in a 'parenty' way, which is different from your way. Everyone does it differently, but as I said before, there's an overall pattern. They need to sort out how best to house, protect and feed their young. They're overwhelmed and, believe me, they're grieving in their own way. Sadly you can sometimes end up feeling like you're invisible! Your sister will feel it too – it's just that she's directing her sadness, anger and hurt into worrying about things like her feather drier in a new tree.

Don't undermine that, understand it; don't beat yourself up, be kind to yourself; don't hurry this process, give yourself time. Your pain will pass and eventually you'll realise it no longer hurts. It can take about a year to really adapt to a new way of life. Total healing can take longer.

Your feelings are normal, so recognising the anger underneath your sadness is OK; notice if you're feeling guilty and remember that this is all part of normal grieving which is an unavoidable process. Just go with the flow and be assured that time will get you through it. Meanwhile, perhaps you could be happy that you all have a new home in the sycamore tree! Look for the positives and think kindly, not selfishly. Your old oak tree was in pain with disease. It's now at peace and you do have a new home! Of course it's OK to cry, but then pick yourself up and know that your feelings are normal and will pass. You just need to understand the process and adapt to your loss and a different way of life."

Tawny was so grateful that he sat up straight and fluffed up his feathers. He felt so much better and could see that his former tree home could not have survived with Sudden Oak Death Disease and it was only fair to let it go. He also remembered that the two-legged beings were right and, to be fair, the one who felled it had, after all, treated the tree which had been their beautiful home for so long with great respect. He thanked Eric and the surrounding crowd for their kindness, support and great wisdom and realised that he could manage his feelings by understanding this grieving process the family had to go through. He also realised that talking things through with friends was a very powerful part of healing.

Eric was now exhausted as the moonlight faded and the stars shone against the black velvety night sky. Everyone dispersed to their homes, reflecting on how loss and separation is something that happens to everything that lives and can be managed when you understand what's happening to you. Feeling much more positive, Tawny took off and flew straight to his new sycamore home, where all that could be seen was a huge ball of hugging feathers as his family welcomed him back to their new house. This had been a great day of learning for Tawny who had found the courage to talk about how he felt and now understood that, even though he was hurting, it was OK to feel that way and that grief is expressed differently by different members of a family.

It was yet another great success for Eric the Oracle, who was now being gently rocked to sleep in his deckchair on his leafy platform by the soft silent movement of the water. He always needed a very big sleep after speaking his great words of wisdom. And so it was this evening. With his silken scarf wrapped cosily around his neck, his monocle nestled in his waistcoat pocket, his dandelion fizzmix glass empty for now, Eric snored and snored through the rest of the night and slept right through until the morning dew covered the land and the early birds broke the silence of the dawn with their welcoming chorus of a new day.

"So remember. When you lose something or someone close to you through death or from them leaving you, grieving for the loss is normal. It's called the grieving process. It starts with the shock at what's happened. Then you'll experience many feelings that can confuse and upset you and you might say or do hurtful things to others when you don't really mean to. Then when you realise your loss is true, you might feel angry or even guilty that you could have done something differently to stop it happening. And throughout all this, you might feel desperately sad. Sometimes it feels like all this is happening at once, but that's what the normal grief process is. Understanding what's happening and sharing how you feel with someone like a friend, someone in your family or someone else that you trust will help you deal with it. Then one day, you will feel better. And so it is."

What have you learned?

_____

_____

_____

_____

_____

_____

_____

_____